A WAY FORWARD FOR HUMANITY
- THE SPIRITUAL BASIS OF THE FINDHORN COMMUNITY.

CAROL RIDDELL

This edition published by Amazon Create Space, 2013.
The author claims copyright over this work.

ey i./ri

Didi

gerhardtd @ gmail. com

Other Books by Carol Riddell:-

The Findhorn Community (1990)
The Path to Love (1996)
Pointers to a Spiritual Life (2013)
Tireragan – a Community on the Ross of Mull
The Chronicles of Thumpus Wumpus – a Story for
Children (with Roy Chillingworth)
The latter three books are available on Amazon
and Amazon Kindle. as is this one.

Introduction.

The Findhorn Community was founded in 1962 by Eileen and Peter Caddy and Dorothy MacLean. Since then is has developed and enlarged itself till it has become a significant spiritual community in the western world, recognised by the United Nations.

In 1990 I published a book, *The Findhorn Community*, sponsored by the community, but representing my own viewpoint on the community. It had a foreword by Eileen Caddy. It sold well, but is now in some respects out of date and is out of print.

In 2012, the Findhorn community celebrated its 50th anniversary. I decided to rewrite the first chapters of the book, concerning the spiritual basis of the community. I have been encouraged by the response to make this short book available to the public, as, unlike the day to day activities of the community, which are constantly developing, they remain stable.

I was a member of the Findhorn Foundation from 1983 - 1990, and of the Erraid Community of the Foundation from 1990 - 1992. I am now part of the wider Findhorn community. With thanks to Carin Schwartz for helping me to locate some of the quotations from Wisdoms, long out of print and especially to Dorothy Maclean who gave me several suggestions to help me modify the material on spiritual guidance, almost all of which I have adopted.

Section 1. The Background

Materialism or Essence - Is the World of Our Senses Real?

Nowadays, most ordinary people learn that the world of our senses is the 'real' world. Growing up in this 'real' world gives rise to desires. The attempt to fulfil them *seems* to give meaning to human existence. Advertising stimulates this view and commercialism provides for it. Materialist philosophies which propose that the world of ordinary sensory perception is the only real one, give it legitimacy. However, the very scientific discoveries that underlie the technological civilisation of our time also indicate that the world of our senses is remarkably limited; best described as a framework allowing a measure of security in an incomprehensible universe, alternatively too vast or too tiny to understand at all.

For example, scientists operate with frequencies of electromagnetic radiation which our senses cannot directly perceive. From them they gain a vastly expanded image of the universe. They use such frequencies as radio waves, microwaves, infrared rays, ultraviolet waves and X-rays. We all know that they exist and that they are used in our technology, but we cannot 'see' them. Each frequency gives a very different picture of the physical world than that of our senses. Which picture is 'true'? If we saw with X-rays, people would appear as skeletons. If we saw with radio waves, they would not seem to exist at all. Our senses provide us with an 'arena for action' they do not tell us the truth.

As you read this, you may feel still and relatively stable. Yet the Earth is spinning on its own axis at 1600 kph at the equator, and moving through space around the sun at 115,000 kph. The sun itself is whirling around the centre of our galaxy at some enormous speed, while the galaxy is moving away from other galaxies even faster. The scale of these movements, the enormous distances which they represent, make our human endeavours seem absolutely infinitesimal. Our senses eliminate almost everything, allowing us to exist comfortably and enabling us to give importance to the little things that surround us. In the great oceans of space we are never still, nor would our endeavours make any impact, even if we managed to destroy life on our planet. On a material level, human existence is actually insignificant. It is only our senses that enable us to build up a delusion to the contrary.

The small end of the spectrum investigated by scientists is equally demoralising for those of us reliant on our senses. Like everybody else, I have a sense of my own physical reality, of that of others and of the world I live in. It, too, appears to be a delusion provided by my sense perception. We descend into the microscopic level of cell, then molecule, then atom. Compressed, the nuclei of the atoms of the human body would cover something like the head of a pin. What remains might be described as energised space. We are nothing more than a pinhead plus energy; poor egos! But techniques have been devised to enable us to 'look at', or infer, the inside of the atomic nucleus itself. Here things become very curious indeed. There is a lot more energised space, and lots of even more infinitesimal 'particles', which, the scientists tell us, may be conceived of 'as if' they were matter or 'as if' they were energy'. Some of these particles or vibrations even appear to be travelling, for short moments, backwards in time, from the future to the past, while others are 'antimatter', perhaps indicating the possibility of a parallel universe, 'in reverse'. One has to use inverted commas to try to translate this reality so that the mind, activated by normal sense impressions, can comprehend it.

Materialist philosophers base themselves on the 'real world'. But this 'real world' is merely an epiphenomenon of the vibratory frequencies ('wavelengths'), on which our senses operate. It is actually the result of an effective way our senses limit what appears to be an endless nothingness orchestrated by constantly changing energy, so that we can exist (relatively) comfortably.

Modern physics and astronomy inform us that we are certainly not what we think we are, and that our efforts are minute in the scale of things. The length of our individual lives is equally minute in the time scale of the universe, although the whole of our physical body, at cellular level, is renewed every eight years. Actually, if one really accepts the discoveries of modern science even up to the present, answers to questions such as 'Who am I?' and 'Why am I?' which are based on our everyday sense impressions seem totally superficial. But the scientists, with all their answers, give us none of the answers. They only make Homo Sapiens seem more and more insignificant, clinging to his little fantasy world. To understand modern scientific discovery itself demands a new level of consciousness, a new structure of intelligence. The world view of Homo Sapiens is no longer adequate to live with the awareness that our sense perceptions tell us but a tiny aspect of truth.

So science actually increases a mystery. It contributes to the anxieties of living if, on top of everything else, we are aware of our utter minuteness in the scale of things, or of the non-material nature of the material. But there has always been another way of looking. It is time for those experiences which have been the property of mystics and 'rishis', the inward-turned wise people of the East, to become the property of us all. For the mystics understood the awesome vastness and minuteness of creation. They knew that everything that seems to be so real is not reality. They found the key that unlocks these secrets and it is time for all of us to put it on our key ring.

By quietening outer activity, including that of the mind, they learned to 'listen' to what is to be 'heard' behind the ordinary sense experience which seems to define our world. They discovered that all the incredible multiplicity of form is an emanation of Oneness. There is an ultimate vibration that underlies all others. It is present everywhere. This vibration consists of what we call LOVE; a love, however, that is unconditional and unattached. No one can prove this to another person; there isn't a machine that can measure it. It has to be experienced. That happens as a result of trying, by seeking it in ourselves, to find what is real, as opposed to what is phenomenal. The techniques for doing this are:- all the various forms of silent meditation and contemplation; training in various kinds of movement and sound; prayer and devotion; and the cultivation of unconditional love in everyday life.

Some physicists have taken note of the writings of the mystics and the oriental sages, because they partly describe the sort of things the scientists investigate. However, the mystics go further. The method of internal enquiry leads to the ultimate truth that Oneness, the Divine Essence, is present everywhere; omnipresent. A conscious attempt to unify with that reality gives life its meaning. Instead of allowing the outer world that we experience to define who we are, we may rather turn inward and discover who we *really* are. *Then* we can learn how to experience the outer world properly and to relate to it blissfully. We can describe this as understanding the outer from the inner, instead of trying to understand the outer from the outer. A spiritual path requires that we learn to make the transition from a world we define by the outer experience of our senses, to one defined by the inner experience of reality. We can then express our discovery in the limited sensory world. It gives that world a different significance, changing the motivation of our actions and ways of relating. Jesus expressed it by calling on us to love our neighbour as ourselves.

In the Findhorn community, we are all, to some degree, encouraged to commit ourselves to this path. Occasionally on the way may come powerful experiences of the truth that Love is the Essence behind form. In modern psychological jargon they are called 'peak experiences'. However, it takes time and spiritual development to 'capture' them; to live consistently from the reality that they express. Time spent in inner space prepares one for the test: what rules in the 'outer' world of our perception; our limited, confusing sense impressions or the inner truth? Our challenges lie in the restricted world of the so-called physical; for to embody truth in this arena we have to be able to see through the delusion of reality that the sense-experienced world presents. Indian teachers have called this delusion '*Maya*', the belief that the limiting experience of sense perception is the truth, instead of a mask over the reality hidden in it.

Finding Reality Inside and Expressing It in the Outer World

In the search for spirit, the meaning of life is twofold. Firstly, we are trying to discover who we really are to experience the Divine within. Secondly, we are trying to express what we discover, through our actions in the perceived world. Such expanded consciousness will enable us to resolve the problems of our current civilisation.

It is not necessary to accept this without question. In order to see whether it is true that the ultimate knowledge of Love lies within you, try adopting the same methods as those who have already discovered it. You will find that you get the same results. The Findhorn Community is an ongoing workshop in which this 'experiment' is being practised. On a spiritual level, that is why it came into existence.

In what way do these views differ from the arguments of established religion? All major religions have two aspects:-

The first propagates belief in the existence of God, and provides a basic moral code for right conduct, righteousness or dharma. This code operates, more or less modified, through social customs and laws. One response to the crises of our times has been to emphasise these outward functions, leading to the growth of fundamentalist movements in both Christianity and Islam.

The second aspect is a mystical current, also present in all religions. The experience of the nature of the Divine is sought through contemplation, or through practices which turn one inward. What is discovered becomes the source of the morality of action. The more you know who you really are, the more your actions will be righteous, for you are expressing Love in the outer world of sense perception.

The world religions have not, up to now, succeeded in preventing any of the world's major crises. This is not because they are essentially wrong, but because they have become 'secularised'. They have emphasised the first, outer aspect of their activity at the expense of the second, inner aspect. As a result, they have accommodated themselves to materialism and its philosophy, rather than providing an alternative, rich way of life. Through this accommodation they have, at least in the West, been reduced in significance in comparison with previous centuries. The present, potentially terminal, crisis of our civilisation requires that the churches emphasise the discovery of God's presence within each of us as the basis of the good life; rather than the pursuit of the material - with a belief in religion added as an ameliorative influence. More people from the established churches are visiting the Findhorn Foundation to experience the effects that even merely a week of working from 'the inside out' has on them.

As we change our orientation to life, so we experience a change in character and in the way we perceive the world. The older mystical philosophies strongly emphasised renunciation, often speaking of the extreme difficulty of the task of discovering inner truth. The state of 'enlightenment', the experience of full embodiment of Divinity, has been confused with the process of spiritual transformation; how one goes about the change. To arrive at a place involves the journey there. Without the journey you cannot arrive. Consciously setting out upon the journey already changes things. Going in the inner direction gives meaning and purpose to life; the more one does it, the more meaning and purpose one finds!

At the beginning of the process of self-discovery, the world of the senses seems to be objective and separate; something to be defended against, or to be overcome. As the experience of inner oneness begins to take hold, this 'objective' world seems to become more flexible, as if it, too, is adjusting itself to the change of emphasis. Strange coincidences begin to occur; the so-called 'real world' starts to relate itself to your new awareness, like a sleeping being slowly awakening. As you go inwards the 'energy frequencies' from which you view things change. The outer world is no longer solid, but begins to dance with you, stimulating you, testing you, assisting you in your transformation. As the inner connection develops further, and awareness deepens, you begin to take the lead in your dance with the world; you gradually become the creator of what happens. A Self oriented towards the Divinity within becomes increasingly able to reshape outer reality. But this Self no longer has the same identity as when it began the transformation; it no longer wants the same things.

The process of reorientation towards inner awareness involves excitement, joy in living, growth in creativity, a relative release of material needs, increased ability to accept people as they are and a determination to resolve problems. The Findhorn community does, to some degree, demonstrate all of these things, which is why so many people want to come to be here. These changes develop the type of identity which humanity needs if we are to survive the present global crisis. This new lifestyle and the requirements for a new civilisation are in harmony.

The Teachings Received by Eileen Caddy and Dorothy Maclean

Both Eileen Caddy and Dorothy Maclean long received messages from an Inner Source. Some of the messages have appeared in their various books. They consistently emphasise that the source of wisdom is to be found within the seeker:

I was shown the earth infilled with great light. I saw that the light was coming up through the earth, infilling every thing and everyone. I felt a tremendous joy and upliftment at what I was being shown. I heard the words, I AM THAT I AM. I AM the alpha and omega and all life. Rejoice, My beloveds, for you are all part of the glorious wholeness, all part of that glorious oneness. (Dawn of Change, p.1)

The only difficulty is in losing yourself that I may be. Do this in the positive way, seeking good wherever you are and seeking Me wherever you can. I am the great aliveness of your being. I am never far away. I answer all calls. I remind you when you want to be reminded. I am within and I am without and the two are increasingly one as you forget your-self and turn to Me. (Wisdoms, p. 13)

Seek and find your direct link with Me. Retain that link no matter what is going on around you. For it is through that link that all things are possible. (Foundations of Findhorn, p. 112)

Relax! Give yourself over completely to Me. There is much to be done but it can be done better in a less desperate hurry. Enjoy everything you do. Savour every action like a connoisseur. Be satisfied only with perfection. (God Spoke to Me, p. 16)

Each soul experiences Me differently but each can find Me within and let Me be prominent in its consciousness. Then, *as I grow more and more important, life is not a separate thing but a part of that consciousness. (*Wisdoms, p. 17*)*

Start this day with 'summit thinking'. Let your thoughts dwell on Me; feel yourself in My presence, walking with Me, talking with Me. Let the wonder of our Oneness sink into your consciousness. Stay in this raised state of consciousness. You can do this when you live fully in the moment, not giving a thought to past moments or future moments but just to this one moment in the Now....

Your close relationship with Me is more important than anything else, for all stems from that relationship. The more time you spend with Me, the smoother will be the running of your everyday living. From that centre, where you will always find Me when you seek, the ripples go out in ever increasing power. (God Spoke to Me, pp. 18,19)

Expand your consciousness and know that I am all there is. Then go on and on expanding it and see the all-inclusiveness of the I AM, and see clearly that you are the I AM of the I AM, that there is no place where I am not. Keep stretching, feel every atom in you ache with stretching, feel yourselves growing, breaking all bonds which have held you in bondage and have stifled your growth and expansion. (Footprints on the Path, p. 96)

Turn within to find all answers, to find all worlds and let our Oneness guide you. (Wisdoms p. 37)

Similar guidance fills their work. When read as a whole, it is clear that through them is being presented not a new theology but a theology which emphasises the 'mystic' connection with Oneness as something available to each of us. This connection is the source of the qualities of a joy-filled life. There is also a strong sense of the inexorability of the process it is an energy transformation whose time has come:-

Step by step My plan is unfolding, and nothing and no one can hold it up. All your needs are being wonderfully met now; all your problems are being solved now; all My wonders are unfolding now. Now is the time. Live fully and gloriously in the ever-present glorious now, and behold Me in everything. (Dawn of Change, p. 13)

You find peace of mind and heart in your nearness to Me. When you are true to Me in you, you are true to all that is true in yourself and there is never a moment's discomfort or doubt in you as to your course, as to what you should be doing, as to the rightness of all your actions. Often the mind hovers about, arbitrating, comparing and preventing your whole-hearted participation in life. Do not let it be your guide; use it as your servant when I have done the guiding. (Wisdoms, p 15)

This is an historic and momentous time in the progress of man. At this time the veil is being rent in two and that which has been hidden through the ages is now to be revealed. The secrets of the sages will no longer be secrets, for all shall know about them. (God Spoke to Me, p. 81)

This is an exacting time for each of you, a time of deep changes within and without, a time of seeking and sorting, of moving into new realms and new dimensions. This period of transition is not easy. You can help by accepting change without resistance . . . . You will see the seemingly impossible become possible, black turned to purest white, evil intent changed in midstream, man at last beginning to see the error of his ways .... He will become awakened at last to the things that really matter in life, the things of the Spirit. (God Spoke to Me, p. 110)

Another major theme in their guidance is that God is Love, and that Love is the essential identity of each individual.

It exists as reality behind all the moods we put on. Knowing that you are Love enables you to see the other as essentially Love, too:-

My love is limitless. Nothing stops the flow of My love except the little self which is free to choose its own way. It turns its back on My love and demands its independence and so cuts itself off. When man chooses to go My way, to walk in My foot steps, the floodgates are released. Once again he can become aware of the wonder of My love. (God Spoke to Me, p. 63)

Beloved, what use is it to love Me within yourself if you cannot love Me within another? As you come to Me within by turning from an awareness of your imperfections, so you come to Me without. When you go around focussed on your own shortcomings or on those of another, then shortcomings are what you will manifest in yourself and what you will see in others and in your environment. (Wisdoms, p 43)

Banish forever all these false teachings and false concepts of Me. I AM love. I AM within each one of you. I AM THAT I AM. (Dawn of Change, p. 145)

Many other contemporary spiritual teachings present the same propositions. It is clear that something important is happening. Humanity is being given a spiritual reorientation course, to enable us to rise to a new level of human interaction. The emphasis in all these teachings is not on the difficulty and unattainability of the goal, but on the immediate benefit of setting out on the path.

All Religions are Ways of Approaching One Truth

In today's world, the parochial belief that there is only one 'true' religion, whose job is to take over all the others, finally has to be abandoned. If God is the Indweller, the reality in us all, then how we seek to discover Him is a matter of cultural background, of personal choice. Our job is to find that means of Self-discovery that best leads us forward from our present starting point. That may lie in Christianity, Hinduism, Islam, Buddhism, Judaism, or some other path. It may be found outside the established practices of the major religions, which, as we have said, often place more emphasis on the promotion of a code of outer social morality than on discovering the basis of morality within. Equally, one may talk of the Indweller as 'God', 'Jehovah', 'Allah', the 'Atman', the 'Essence', the 'Oneness behind all diversity', or the 'Christ Consciousness'. What we find does not differ; the various names and forms in worship are labels and practices to help us.

We are being asked to adjust to a world situation in which, for survival's sake, we need to learn that culturally and spiritually we are like flowers in a garden, each with its own particular shape, colour and fragrance, each equally valid. We can no longer judge other cultures or religions as either better or worse than our own. In recent years the Findhorn Foundation has consciously chosen to be an international community. The validity of each person's method of finding their path to the inner truth is accepted. Our relative success demonstrates that it can be done.

Ignorance is the Basis of Evil

The idea of God as the Essence, the Reality of all that is, omnipresent and omniscient, is a monistic one. There is only God, only the 'Atma' or Essence. Everything that seems otherwise is the result of the way it is viewed, not its reality. The notions of evil and sin and their accompanying feelings of guilt have led to a widespread sense of inadequacy and worthlessness. But ultimate Good is not a quality that can be defined by its relationship to that which is perceived as Not Good, its negation. It is, simply, the truth, that which *is*. The opposite of that which is, is that which is not, i.e. non-existent. There is therefore only Good, and its discovery is the discovery of the truth. That which is not good, i.e., evil, is not something different from the Divine, an alternative, inherently evil universal force but *behaviour without a knowledge of the truth*. The devil does not lie outside us, hoofed and horned; he represents that in us which has not discovered the truth, and therefore does not act from truth, but from ignorance. The temptation of Christ, for instance, does not involve some nasty being approaching Him and offering Him the things of the world in place of those of the spirit. It lies in His own inner temptations to lose God-consciousness and take the material world for reality, desires which substitute the ephemeral for the real. Jesus did not succumb to these temptations, and today we also have to learn to resist them.

By arriving at this understanding, 'wrong action' may be defined in three ways:-

-Action in contradiction to the laws of society may, in the short term, seem to bring material benefits.

19

-Action in contradiction to divinely revealed laws, such as the Ten Commandments, is usually accompanied by guilt and inner conflict, but may also seem to bring material benefits.

-However, action in which the Real is confused with the Unreal stems from loss of identity with the Divine, the Indweller. Sai Baba gives an example:- in the half dark (*ignorance or confusion*) you may mistake a piece of rope for a snake. Then you act inappropriately (*evil or fear*). If you take a light (*seek truth*), you will see that it is not a snake but a rope, and be able to act appropriately (*know who you really are*). Loss of identity with truth leads to a sense of meaninglessness, of inner despair.

Many lost people turn to drugs to try to find a moment of truth amidst the meaninglessness they experience, and they destroy their lives in their desperation to recapture bliss. We need to help one another to regain consciousness of the truth we may have momentarily perceived but then turned away from.

Embodied Self, Soul Self and Real Self

A view very widely held in the Findhorn Community is that of the separation of the identity of body and soul. When we talk of life we are referring to three aspects, as if they were on different 'frequencies':-

-Individual life in the body;

-The 'life' of the soul, using individual incarnations as a means of training in self -discovery;

'-Eternal life', that the soul is in the process of discovering the universal, unchanging, timeless Essence, Divinity itself.

If we understand that what we think of as matter results from the way that our sense organs limit our experience, the concept of a non-material soul, entering and re-entering the physical world, becomes much easier to envisage. Indeed, the medieval Christian view of a soul existing in a body only once, and then being sent to heaven, hell or purgatory for eternity on the basis of that one life seems naive. The idea of reincarnation has been a keynote of the Hindu religion, and was current in very early Christianity. Paths to self-discovery provide too much evidence of previous existence in human form to be denied out of hand.

Each individual personality is largely unaware of its earlier existences but, on the inward path, there are opportunities for enhanced memory of such incarnations, which may be applied so as to release blockages in present life. Such recall has even been used as the basis of historical novels, and can be available under deep hypnosis. As these 'memories' are experienced, it appears that we are not merely our current identity but *a soul in development*, operating through many incarnations in the material frequencies of the sense organs and learning from the law of cause and effect (karma). The consequences of wrong actions that we perform from ignorance return to us as lessons, giving us a chance to seek another way. At some time everyone has experienced lives lost in the illusion of immediate gratification or dominated by the energy of base passions. People who have had a problem and resolved it are often much more understanding of someone who is currently going through a similar difficulty. When we learn that we, as souls, are not merely 'saints' but have also been 'sinners', it helps with a higher level of compassion to assist those still living in confusion.

In the Findhorn community, of course, no one is asked to believe in reincarnation in order to become a member or to visit us; we have few dogmas! But people are asked to search for the God within. As their awareness expands, they usually begin to experience something of their 'soul self' and its previous incarnations. There is no point, however, in dwelling overmuch on the past when the present is so exciting, or on the partial when the whole is available.

With the realisation that divinity is indweller, 'true self', omnipresent, its nature unconditional love; that the purpose of life is the soul's conscious reunion with its truth; that the physical reality of this world is the stage on which the ongoing drama of life (as well as death and suffering) is set, the meaning of our lives comes to be perceived as something very different than it is if we mistake the material world of our senses for reality. Death becomes the conclusion of a particular scene in the drama; birth the opening of one. Suffering results from taking the phenomenal world as real, and compassion gives others assistance on their path to truth. Seen in this way, life is a wonderful, ever-changing adventure, and one can gradually become filled with inner happiness and peace. On the way, life is more interesting and enjoyable, there is less worry, and more care about others.

Materialism encourages people to seek fulfilment in the external world, either through what they do, or through what or whom they possess. They experience themselves as limited and needy people, whose requirements have to be met in order for them to be happy. They are subject to unhappiness if they do not have what they think they need, or if something is taken away, or if their performance is criticised. Strength for them involves qualities of aggression or dominance. Their endeavours are directed towards controlling, or defending themselves from, the environment. If they are religious, they tend to believe in an external God who regulates their conduct through a revealed moral code. Many do not find the satisfaction they seek in the external world, and may be frustrated and sometimes bitter. These are *outer-directed people*, individuals characteristic of the civilisation we are leaving behind.

People who centre their lives on the discovery of inner truth tend to see their needs as transient and the things they have as secondary; the experienced world reflects to them what they need to transform in themselves to find who they really are. As they discover new aspects of themselves, they are excited to share them. They find life fulfilling and exciting, but sometimes suffer from impatience, very conscious of the gap between their present state and where they hope to go. They find strength in calmness and clarity of vision. The things of the material world are a means, not an end, to them. Their religion is inward-directed and contemplative; they tend to seek transcendental states, and in their behaviour they attempt to communicate the experience of these states to others.

These *inner-directed* people are developing the characteristics necessary for a human civilisation which will, one hopes, replace our present one. The Findhorn community is about the development of such individuals.

Section 2. The Need for Personal Transformation

Individual Frustration in a Materialist Society

A social value system in which success is defined in terms of ability to get to the top is built on an obvious paradox. There are only a certain number of positions of wealth, power and influence. No matter how clever, ambitious or able people are, they cannot all be political leaders or captains of industry. As the old saying goes, 'you can't put a quart into a pint pot', and the fact that most people won't reach the 'top' has nothing to do with their own individual abilities, but simply reflects the reality of social organisation itself. Accepting an ideology based on such a contradiction is bound to create frustration. Some have a measure of success and consider themselves superior. Others bemoan their fate as less adequate human beings. Some try to opt out into an escapist dream of drugs, or into an endless, meaningless observation of the activities of those ('celebrities' - fantasy people) provided for them by television and the internet. Yet others try to satisfy their frustrated ambitions in non-legitimate ways, turning to the criminal world to seek fame and fortune.

In societies which called themselves socialist, the vision of 'true communism' was unable to mobilise enough of the idealism needed for collective action, except during short periods when material frustrations with the old order boiled over. A world of propagandistic make-believe was created in which people became cynical about everything. At the end, the leaders of the Soviet Union called for spiritual regeneration. Mikhail Gorbachov compared his vision of socialism to a 'temple on a green hill'; just as the entire façade of 'socialist' Eastern Europe collapsed like a house of cards. Neither socialist nor capitalist materialism has provided real human satisfaction.

It cannot be said that even those who derive the greatest material benefit from our current social structures have found much fulfilment. A new car is a joy, but not forever. The pleasure of a second new car palls more rapidly. So it is with material wealth in general; the pleasures it provides are of diminishing value. Of course, it is pleasant not to have to worry about material needs. The unhappiness of the wealthy, however, provides a hunting ground for therapists. The dream of material wealth has been an effective stimulus, working on the most primitive levels of desire, but its realisation does not live up to its promise.

As the scale of modern society grows and it becomes increasingly transnational in scope, more and more people feel powerless and frustrated. Mass housing developments provide unbelievably unstimulating environments to live in. People may undergo bouts of mental or psychosomatic illness and withdraw by opting out, or project their bitterness onto those nearby who seem different. Racism, religious and nationalist fanaticism, football violence and hooliganism are all symptomatic of a sense of disempowerment that, in appropriate circumstances, erupts into extremist political movements. Democratic choice is often confined to the occasional right to vote in increasingly huge constituencies for representatives who themselves are not necessarily close to any real decision-making. Modern therapeutic movements have developed many techniques for encouraging personal development, but, all too often, these methods are used in vain attempts to help people adjust to ways of living with fundamentally unsatisfying values.

It is unlikely that this kind of alienated lifestyle, reflecting an increasingly common, crisis-ridden social situation, can be modified to provide human satisfaction. People can best begin to transcend such a state through the discovery and development of connection with the source of all, the 'indweller', the divine reality underlying all forms and present in each of us. Then life becomes meaningful, empowerment develops and effective action can be taken within any social situation. Our job in the Findhorn community is to explore this change. In this way we can assist people in their transition from a world view which has become inadequate to cope with the situation on the planet, to one which gives both individual satisfaction and the personal resources for the wider social changes our civilisation needs.

Changing 'Human Nature'

As we transform ourselves, learning to work from within, traditional, external morality ceases to be a rule by which we ought to act, but becomes a guide as to whether our inward listening is effective. For, as we start the process of working from 'the inside out', we immediately come up against all the old ways of thinking and behaving with which we have lived for years and which are very familiar to us. They can be described as the personality as we know it, or, our everyday sense of self.

It is the transformation of this everyday self into the 'Self within' which provides the challenge of the new spirituality. The transformation needs to be dealt with delicately and lovingly, but it needs to be dealt with. Some seekers may undergo an overwhelming experience of what it means to be real, but even such glimpses, while intensely motivating, are usually brief. The task is to embody the experience, to create an identity and a lifestyle that express it. For this inner work, support and guidance is needed. That is why, in the Findhorn community, we support each other and use all sorts of techniques, including therapy and self-development workshops, to move along this path. Our aim is not to adjust to the old, but to facilitate the discovery of the truth behind appearances, and to live from that.

One of the conditions of human development is that we must use survival strategies. We are born innocent and unconditionally loving, but helpless, without the ability either to look after ourselves or to communicate anything other than the most basic needs. The love that we receive in return, however, is by no means totally unconditional. It is mixed up with our parents' conception of how we ought to be. In turn the child's unconditional love is modified. The result of this ongoing interaction provides the dynamic of personality formation. If demands are too difficult for a child to accommodate, he or she may in the most extreme cases be battered in frustration by a parent and die. A child who is expected never to cry or to be nothing other than a sweet living doll, may develop a mutilated personality and emerge as an adult suffering from deep frustration and inner rage. But, extremes apart, each person as a little child has had to evolve a strategy for coping with not-well understood demands from the parental world.

Many of these strategies, dating from the earliest pre-verbal levels, become adopted unconsciously and structure a developing identity. It is not merely, for instance, that we may feel unloved. Little children may, in their innocence, define non-love as if it were love, and spend their lives seeking the rejection they experienced from their parents. It is, for them, the only real satisfaction, although as adults they are merely aware that their relationships 'go wrong'. Some, seeking to please, come to feel that they are real only when they do what others want. As they begin to try to discover who they really are, they may experience a deep angst, as if there is actually nothing to them at all.

As we progress from being babies to children, what we actually want, basic love and nutrition, becomes differentiated and defined in our developing consciousness:- we want sweet foods, we cling to Mummy, and so on. We take into ourselves, through our parents and other significant figures, the ideas of satisfaction prevalent in our culture. They do not seem to belong to others; they are 'ours' - what we like or don't like, what gives us pleasure, what gives us pain. Much of our self-evaluation, our judgement of ourselves, our levels of self-confidence, aggressiveness, insecurity is actually an internalization of other people's views, accepted before we had the ability to evaluate them. Adults may find comfort in the belief in

God's forgiveness of us as sinners; we may use a strict moral code to hold all our deep frustrations and violent impulses in check; we may use our reason to try to provide explanations for why we behave as we do, and to ameliorate the judgements that crowd in on us; but we all tend to react against an essentially imported concept of self that we have unconsciously adopted as our own. So we get by, adapting with more or less success to the immense changes going on around us, living a life of pleasure and pain, satisfaction and frustration as our survival patterns are constantly activated and reactivated.

There is, however, a deep yearning built into our identity. Psychologists tend to call it a 'curiosity drive', which lies at the root of all the strategies described above. Such yearning can underlie, for example, compulsive acquisitive behaviour, though it is never satisfied by it. I want: women; men; cars; a yacht; everything to be in order; freedom; pleasure; excitement; to be noticed; and so on. The 'I want' is their root. It underlies them all. In fact, what I want is to know who I am. Finally, nothing else will do. Either I die frustrated and the search goes on; or fulfilled, merged with the divine source. Eileen and Dorothy's inner source says:

As you raise your consciousness and realise your Oneness with Me, there is no duality. Love flows through you in ever-increasing power, and you see only the perfect and good in all. How necessary it is for you to do this. Really understand that mankind is made in My image and is therefore perfect. If I am your Father, I am the Father, Mother, God of all mankind. Accept this realisation. (God Spoke to Me, p. 77)

Unless you come to Me in the silence and attune to Me, you go through life without the slightest idea of who you are. You can go through life with the idea of yourself based on your education, which merely reflects world consciousness and is very mental, based on what you see in the mirror, which

29

is but the outer form, based on your emotional reactions to others which is totally misleading and limited by all manner of things. You are not what you think and feel you are and yet you perform all your life as if you were - and all the while what you truly are is right here, radiating harmony out to all the worlds from the centre of you. (Wisdoms, p.51)

To acknowledge this deep yearning, a personal shift in identity from the sense of ourselves that we learned in our psychological process of development, towards our essence, who we really are, is necessary. It is actually the reason why the Findhorn community is here, and why it is so successful. For anybody can make such a change, whether they be rich or poor, intellectual or practical, complicated or simple, believer or agnostic; whatever their nationality or religion. And, as they change, the great 'I want', father of all the other 'I wants', begins to be satisfied, and life becomes exciting and fulfilling. As the change is made, the problems of alienation and disempowerment diminish. We slowly become calmer, stronger, clearer. We begin to release our frustrations, we grow less needy, less compulsive. A calmer, more loving, aware and considerate identity begins to emerge.

This process is the social 'paradigm shift' that humanity has to make to overcome the problems which beset us. Furthermore, it is not only the successful completion of this task which is fulfilling. The attempt to change, itself, provides a full agenda for life. Far from attempting to escape from a dispiriting reality, we engage with life because it is so interesting. There is so much to be done; doing it is so exciting!

In the Findhorn community we live without major stress in a beautiful environment but we are very busy. The days are always too short. Developing a relationship with the Real involves a new relationship with all that one has known, seeing it with new eyes, ones that become increasingly more loving and compassionate and less judgmental. On the journey to the Self, we are assisted by two kinds of techniques:

The first techniques relate to inner development, and many of them are meditative in quality. "*Be still*," said the Voice to Eileen, "*and know that I am God.*" Such techniques, which can be adapted for simple group work, take one on the journey inwards, to the 'higher' self. Contrary to common belief, they are not difficult or demanding, and do not have to be undertaken for hours at a time. Their purpose is the discovery of Love within. To go deeper into meditation techniques is a personal decision which may be made as one becomes aware of the benefits they bring. If it is undertaken as a result of other people's opinions there will be an inner conflict which presents itself when one becomes still. Inner discipline develops as a means, not as an end in itself, but it does require application. In this, it is no different from the discipline required to acquire a skill. You cannot be a musician, a doctor or a carpenter without training. Why should the ultimate skill require none?

The second set of techniques is for when we get stuck; for when we are afraid to let go of the old. They make use of a variety of therapeutic practices. At the Findhorn community we use anything that works, and there are usually qualified practitioners available. But the use of these techniques is a means, not an end in itself. The community is not a therapy centre, and therapy is not the solution to the human predicament. The aim is to release anything that blocks us from becoming Self-identified (rather than selfish), as quickly and as economically as possible. We are trying to find the Love that lives in us, and with freeing ourselves to embody it in an ever-increasing quantity. The challenge is to practise what is found. To pretend to be loving when one does not feel it is the utmost hypocrisy. When we find that we are not feeling loving, it is sensible to investigate what is blocking the love, and to use an appropriate technique to release the block. In this way, step by step, the psychological structure of the identity can be re-formed.

Reason as Servant, not Master

Another aspect of the process of restructuring the identity to come 'from the inside out' involves reconsidering attitudes to reason. Reason is the mechanism by which we learn to give order to the incomprehensibility of the world. It is the basic working tool for the understanding of phenomenal experience. By learning to predict what will happen when we act, we acquire some measure of control over our environment. But reason soon becomes a tyrant instead of a servant. For, as well as enabling some control over the world we experience, our developing reason begins to limit what 'can' happen. "What is not seen can't be real," it says. "What we know with our senses is the only truth." The objectivity of the view of the world that our senses give us has already been challenged. And we have talked of guidance, channelling, 'going within' to help discover a wider reality. None of these are available if we adhere strictly to a definition of the world propounded by reason. Neither Eileen's nor Dorothy's guidance, nor the founding of the Findhorn Foundation are easily explained by reason.

To find who we are, we have to learn to put our critical faculty on hold. It is too dependent on inadequate definitions of what is real. Many people are rather fearful of this. Reason, for them, seems to keep their unresolved, unconscious desires at bay and guards against possible craziness. It is not to deny our existence in the phenomenal world. But, rather than being the determinant of truth, that world provides the framework in which incarnated beings operate. As such, it is an excellent 'reality check'. The behaviour of deluded people will not spread love and wisdom, but unhappiness for themselves and others. Such people have not found the frequency of truth, but have lost themselves in another level of illusion.

In spirituality, reason has its place, not to limit reality, but as a checking mechanism which enables a relationship to be made between claims and results. Divine Grace as well as intuitive modes of seeking knowledge operate through the physically-experienced world, where the consequences of their application can be checked. But without the extra qualities of grace and intuition, the door to self-discovery is locked. The innumerable 'coincidences' which happen at the Findhorn community also quickly undermine the overweening rule of reason. One, or even two, coincidences can be accepted as such, but when they come in a stream, we must, if we are 'reasonable', begin to allow for the possibility that 'reality' is much more flexible than our reason can envisage.

A small model illustrates this way of describing human identity:

DIVINE SELF
(Who I really am)
⋂

A HIGHER SELF
(Getting there!)
⋂

(Spiritual development techniques)
PAST EXPERIENCE |PERSONALITY | FUTURE SEEKING
(May need releasing (My current sense of myself |(May make

-Regression work) | -who I think I am) | me anxious)

(Therapy techniques)
⋓
UNCONSCIOUS
(Keeps tripping me up)

Our perceived self — who we think we are — with its three aspects, is in centre position. Below it are our unconscious wishes, or impulses, which we may uncover with therapeutic techniques. On the left side is our past, not just that of our current life, but an immense area of experience in other lives. It may occasionally be useful to become aware of aspects of this through past-life regression techniques. On the right is our future which we can usually only seek to know about. Time is the best agent for discovering this aspect of ourselves, though we may get some indication as to general trends and problems from astrologers and clairvoyants, though much of this work can be bogus. Above is our Higher Self and above that the Divine Self.

By contacting the Higher Self we can understand the world of our perceptions, and look at our problems in a new way. Moving in this 'upward' (inner) direction constitutes the spiritual path. None of the areas that lie outside the self experienced personality, the ego-self, are immediately apparent, but they are very real. The search for an inclusive identity gives humanity its true raison d'être. We will just have to do it, in order to cope with the monstrous problems of our materialist, externally directed civilisation.

The Energy of Transformation

If we look at a candle burning in a darkened room, we can see its flame. But the candle also lights the room. If we look at a computer screen, we can see what is written there. But the computer screen also gives out energy (the 'tempest' effect) and it can be read at a distance with the appropriate equipment. Firms worry that people can steal their secrets that way! In both cases, an energy is being given out. In the first case we can see the flame; we also see by the light emitted. In the second case we can see what's on the screen, but not the emitted energy. When we have an X-ray, we cannot see anything, still, the energy may have an effect on us.

By extension, it is not too difficult to imagine that everything we are and do gives off energy. When someone is angry, for instance, our senses observe the way they behave; from that we infer that they are angry. We cannot see the energy they give off, but we may feel uncomfortable and want to keep out of the way; or our own angry feelings may be triggered and we respond in kind. Sometimes we may feel angry for no apparent reason, triggered by the energy of the anger of someone else, whom we can't see. Psychologists have spent much effort trying to prove that these effects are solely the results of observable stimuli. It is a bit like saying that there isn't anything but the flame of the candle; that it doesn't give off any light. Of course, we can see by the light, so we can't deny that an energy is radiated that affects us. Because we can't see the energy of an angry person, it doesn't mean that it isn't there, or that it doesn't affect us.

If there is a nuclear accident, such as that at Fukushima, we do not at the time see or feel anything, but irradiated particles from material released are carried by the wind and their energy is received by our bodies. In a shorter or longer time, depending on the dose, physical effects will result: depression, sickness, hair loss, long-term cancer. We cannot usually feel the energies that human beings give out, but they also have effects on us, for good or ill. As soon as we grasp this, we can move beyond two delusions.

- The first delusion is that what we do involves merely the physical acts that we perform, the words that we utter, the expressions we put on. Actually, whatever we do gives off energy vibrations, which are picked up by others and affect them, quite apart from our ordinary means of communication.

- In the second delusion we think that what is not expressed is not communicated. But thoughts, feelings and states of being also give off energies. They are received by others in an analogous way to radioactivity although we have not developed sense receptors that allow us to be immediately aware of them.

Spiritual teachers have constantly advised us to keep good company and to 'clean up' our mental state, because they know that negative energies are transmitted and do have an effect. If our life strategies have left us with unresolved inner conflicts, that energy will slowly undermine our physical and mental health. It will also tend to make others uncomfortable around us, or perhaps draw to us those who have similar problems, or who in order to feel real or worthwhile, need people to 'heal'. A materialistically oriented civilisation generates many people with such conflicts. They are inwardly frustrated individuals who radiate such an energy outwards.

A group of unhappy people radiates a more powerful energy of unhappiness than an unhappy individual. A group of angry people does the same; a group of loving people likewise. Human energy waves spread themselves out from their source, as light spreads from a candle flame. A group of people who are living in the attempt to discover and express inner truth will give off a different energy than a group of people who are striving to fulfil themselves by acquiring possessions. The energies given off by people who are pretending to be fulfilled when they are not, differ from those their observed behaviour indicates. The energies radiated by a group of fundamentally happy people may be attractive to a group of unhappy ones, even though they may never actually meet.

All this is rather important in understanding the working of the major transformation of which our community is a part. We can describe what has been done physically here, who has come and gone, how people live together, and how endless groups of people who come experience a change of consciousness. But all these interactions involve small numbers in comparison with, say, a football crowd. A major significance of the Findhorn community is in the energies it generates, and in the energies that those who visit us generate. Fulfilled people have an influence on unfulfilled people, even if the latter do not visit us or meet someone who has. Such people will not know anything about the community, but gradually a feeling that there is something better, that there is another way, that there is hope, may surface. People are drawn inwards; ideas suddenly become current that were previously 'cultist' - such as, those affirming that for life to become meaningful, the divine is to be sought within.

A candle light may be too dim for us to see by; an arc light may be so bright that it dazzles us. To be able to see well and comfortably, we need a light of just the right brightness. Some people have eyes that can stand strong light; other people's eyes are weak, so they need a gentler light. In a similar way, the quality of energy given off by supreme spiritual teachers may be too powerful for many people. The reaction can be, "They are wonderful, but they are not like me. I couldn't be like that." The energies given off by a group of people like the Findhorn community are not so powerful; they come from fulfilled people, but not perfect ones. The effect is like a soft, pleasant light. Our task is to make sure that our energy emanations are not too weak for people to feel them, nor too strong for people to relate personally to them.

The Findhorn community generates energy at a particular vibrational frequency. We work in conjunction with other centres and individuals, some of which are 'brighter' than us, others less bright. We are drawn towards the brighter ones, and the others are drawn towards us. In this way we are part of a network of energy transformation on the planet which is spreading more widely and steadily increasing in power. Using the symbolism of light, which is common to all religions, we call it a 'Network of Light'.

The community is not just an ordinary place in which our personal energies alone are generating a transformative urge. There is an energy source here which amplifies the energy we generate, so that we resemble a transmitter. One proof of this is the way the community came into being. We often call this source the 'Angel of Findhorn', and it is one of a number of special energy sources which appear to be operating for the transformation of the planet. The energy present in the community tends to stimulate us to change ourselves, so that most of us are often challenged here. This is our conscious or unconscious choice. We tend to attract people for whom our energy level is 'right', but the community as a whole is also in change, so that the energies working through us are becoming more diverse.

The development of humanity will not come about by the slow multiplication of people seeking a new lifestyle. There is reason to posit a 'threshold level', beyond which new consciousness will simply 'be there' for everyone. When enough people have 'found the way', everybody will 'know' that the meaning of life is to be found in the search for the Divine within. It will become the new orthodoxy! Humanity will be able to solve its problems and live with a degree of mutual love, harmony and acceptance, caring for the planet as a whole. Of course, it is hoped that this happens before humanity destroys itself under the pressure of the problems its disoriented civilisation has created.

In the Findhorn community the general view is that there is indeed time to reach a positive critical mass. This is because of the awareness that it is not 'just us'. Divine grace is stimulating the change. We, among many others, are playing our part in reaching the transformation point, not only by personal transformation but by learning to support the energy that is available here to flow out through us to the world.

Section 3. A Spiritual Symbol for Western Humanity?

The Findhorn Community: An Accessible Model for Change

To express divinity fully in daily life is no easy task but, as one begins to try, dramatic changes can be made in the quality of living, in happiness and in comprehension of individual and world events. We become involved in a reorientation of our lives which has immediate, concrete results. This is important because many spiritual books imply that such changes cannot take place without enormous self-sacrifice, harsh discipline and total renunciation. Perhaps the efforts of earlier spiritual seekers have opened a door for us, through which, with grace, we can now pass much more easily.

In the last 50 years, the Findhorn community has developed an approach to spirituality which requires no more effort than needed to learn any complex skill. Yet it is effective in developing a level of human consciousness that might bring us through humanity's present crises to a higher stage of human interaction. It could enable us to live in relative harmony with one another and in a much more positive connection with the physical world around us. Such a transformation is available to all, now. It can give people a feeling of purpose and direction in their lives which, on a world scale, would do away with racial, social, religious and nationalist intolerance and with gross economic exploitation. It creates awareness of common humanity, and leads to more fulfilled and happier lives for everyone. A big return for a relatively modest investment!

A sceptic may be resistant. Is this not just hype, idealistic theorising, self-delusion born of naiveté? How can it be known that such things are possible? At one moment we proclaim dramatic changes in human identity and at the next, talk of easy transitions!

The Findhorn community is not an ideal, a vision, a high-sounding theory, or even a blueprint for transformation. There is no pretence to have a recipe for instant perfection; nor are we a community of recluses, living in retreat from the day-to-day world. The community is an ongoing, practical, working example of how a degree of transformation can occur in relatively ordinary individuals within a short period of time. Such a transformation involves a lifestyle whose positive results can be assessed and measured by any social scientist or, more importantly, by any interested inhabitant of the planet. Furthermore, our origins and background are a clear and convincing demonstration of divine intent; something is being created here for a special purpose. One of the most widely read books about the Findhorn community was called *The Magic of Findhorn*. Its journalistic style tended to emphasize the more extraordinary aspects of early community life, and some of the special characters who were initially drawn here, but there *is* a 'magic' in the community, a divine magic. Its function is to stimulate us to perform the tasks for which we have been attracted here.

The Findhorn community was not founded as the result of a rational discussion among rational people about creating a new group of rational human beings. Our civilisation exalts rationality as the answer to world problems, but it is the 'age of reason' that has brought us to today's state of crisis. As bread needs the leaven of yeast, so, for positive change, rationality needs the leaven of intuitional inspiration. Perhaps there is a plan in place, of which our rational selves have no knowledge, a plan that is not, in a normal sense, human in origin and which has its own sense of timing.

Eileen and Dorothy received guidance in meditations. Over a period of years, they became used to the messages they received. Nothing happened in a hurry. Eileen's autobiography, *Flight into Freedom*, gives the distinct impression that a plan slowly unfolded. Guidance was given to prepare for events that later came to pass. The Caddy family and Dorothy Maclean found themselves, as predicted by the guidance, apparently rejected, in a tiny caravan facing a rubbish dump in an uninspiring sandy caravan park in north-east Scotland. The messages began to provide instruction after instruction as to how to proceed. Because Peter Caddy followed Eileen's more specific instructions and those of Dorothy, who found she was able to communicate with the energies controlling plant growth, their new garden started to produce enormous vegetables, attracting international attention to the emerging community.

Even then things were not hurried. After David Spangler's arrival in 1970, and partly through his channelled writing, did the world-wide significance of the Findhorn community become apparent to those outside esoteric circles. Spangler's inner teachers related the meaning of the developing community to the solution of world problems, and his impetus supported expansion. The main focus began to be redirected, emphasizing more spiritual education of people, the transformation of human beings. Often, at the beginning, the humans involved in these changes were uncertain of their direction. Eileen and Dorothy's messages gave them the direction and understanding to help them to go forward. The story of the early days of the community is exciting and inspiring. Inner attunement through meditation, in conjunction with the signs the world is giving, is a better means of making decisions than the application of reason alone.

For instance, one of the great contributions a group of people can make to our society at the present time is to divorce the idea of happiness from that of material wealth. This is not done by pious theorising about the 'sanctity of poverty', but by demonstrating a way of living which, while not renouncing material things, is not dependent on them. Even though objects may not be new and expensive, if they are loved and cared for, they shine out those qualities for others to enjoy. There is no enthusiasm to retain things which are too old to be effective, but it is surprising how much more service a loved and cared-for machine will give than one that is not. The material achievements of the community, while modest, give an impression that is quite out of proportion to their scale and cost.

Turning within demands some kind of spiritual practice. To find it is the first hurdle to overcome as one seeks to change the 'frequency' of life. A few people who become members have maintained a strict discipline of meditation over preceding years, and it is surprising how such people tend to give up these habits once they live in the Findhorn Foundation - at least for a time. The emphasis is on inner discipline, not one imposed from outside, even when one's own conscience is the imposer. Conscience may merely be the internalised voice of external authority. A sense of duty may help a person through a difficult patch in their transformation, but if it remains the basis of their spirituality, the identity is still outer-directed. Truth even transcends conscience.

Others come seeking to turn inwards; but someone who has been prepared to spend hours mending a car or absently watching a television screen may find it a challenge to learn to spend even half an hour a day being still. Relatively, however, attaining inward quiet requires such a small effort. Initially, a personal spiritual practice might not even involve much quiet meditation. It could centre on a movement discipline, like T'ai Chi, or even regular conscious appreciation of nature. We do encourage everyone to develop some practice which helps them to be inwardly still.

The nurturing and expression of love is another, very important kind of spiritual practice. When this involves people to whom we are attracted, it seems easy, but such love is very conditional. At the Findhorn Foundation, people are constantly coming and going. A loving feeling no sooner develops than the person towards whom it is directed leaves. Gradually, one learns to love in a less conditional way. Ultimately, everything centres around learning to love, for unconditional love expresses our Divine nature.

At the same time as encouraging individual spiritual practice, the community has developed its own small rituals of silence and inner connection. These, though imposing no heavy burden on the participants, both remind and enable us to change focus from 'normal' outward directed life. Attendance at daily collective meditations is encouraged but not obligatory. The members of each work department meditate together weekly, and community meetings always include a meditation. Work periods begin with a moment of silent awareness, in which hands are held in a circle. Many members bless the commencement and completion of special tasks with a meditation. These small rituals provide the basis of a life in the initial process of turning inwards, and require very small amounts of determination and perseverance. The immediate results of calmness and increased group harmony they bring give a stimulus to go further. They support but do not force inner development.

As we experience the divine in ourselves, we become aware that it exists in everyone else, too. God is omnipresent.

We realise that in order to express love, we must remove the barriers to doing so. We begin to see that those who do not express love are merely stuck behind barriers they themselves have erected for 'protection'. We can regard them with more understanding and support them in finding the confidence they need to take the barriers down. Each person has to work at his or her own pace, for people who are under pressure usually feel threatened and tend to close up.

In this great spiritual adventure, judgement is slowly replaced by comprehension. Judgement breeds punitiveness and gossip, as destructive of self-development as it is of the development of others. Comprehension, on the other hand, stimulates mutual support in change and transformation. Further, we gradually come to recognise that Divinity is as much the essence of the material world as of the human one. This is why we give names to the tools and machines with which are used.

All these practices are aspects of 'positive thinking'. Positive thinking includes seeking to be aware of a reality underlying the apparent. It does not mean trying to run away from or deny that which is difficult, tedious or challenging. To try to pretend that things are good when they are difficult is merely a symptom of being controlled by fear.

Findhorn community lifestyle is not retreatist. The aim is to present the 'good news' of our Self-discovery and to maintain it in the daily practice of a working community. A new, positive meaning in work is being explored, not only in what is done, but in how it is done and the way it is shared with others. This is expressed by the phrase 'Work is love in action!' To begin to experience work in this way is often very revealing for guests, who may discover that they can find satisfaction in tasks they previously regarded as menial and mundane. As the currently dominant social desires to maximise material gain and output are superseded, people become used to working in an economy of sufficiency. Our perspective on work, which includes discussion and mutual sharing, decentralisation and democratisation of authority, could gradually transform working life. Changed attitudes to work are not a means by which greedy employers can extract more output from individuals. The approach fostered in daily life at the Findhorn community is part of a transformation of working situations and values. The aim is to move in the direction of a world characterised by caring and mutual respect.

Cultural and Religious Integration

From its outset, the Findhorn community has been an international one. Dorothy, a Canadian, shared the earliest years with Peter and Eileen, who were English, and with Lena who was Scottish. At present the community contains people from many countries and cultures but, up to now, mainly from wealthy 'Western' societies the heartland of materialistic civilisation. Challenge and stimulation from other cultures helps to expand limited assumptions about reality. To guests, our practice seeks to demonstrate that cultural difference can be transcended in everyday living and that the world unification process created by communications technology can be experienced positively.

Up to now, our particular function in a world-wide movement of change is to work with people from the 'exporter' nations of materialism - those nations whose cultures emphasise material possession as the most desirable human value rather than with people from the 'importer' nations - those whose spiritual heritage has been undermined by such values. This 'Westernness' has been a challenge for many. We are aware of the plight of the poor of the world, and of the dedicated and self-sacrificing efforts made by both religious and secular organisations to alleviate poverty and starvation. It is a challenge to conscience to justify working with relatively wealthy people in a task of personal spiritual transformation, when there is so much material deprivation to be found. But one has to come to the conclusion not only that every human being is inherently divine and worthy of transformation, but also that the real root of the problem of poverty lies in the destruction of a spiritual core to life in the so-called 'advanced industrial societies' themselves.

Spiritual richness and material richness often represent alternative world value systems. While the 'advanced' societies may be the centre of material wealth, they are sometimes the backward nations of spiritual wealth. Many cultures are spiritually much richer than ours. From this perspective, the Findhorn community's work could be described as missionary work. Without such efforts our societies will continue to export cultural destruction and very possibly extinction itself to the rest of humanity.

With the proper use of resources, the elimination of the grosser extremes of poverty in the world is no impossible task. To this end it is crucial to transform the value systems of our societies, societies that have lost much of the vitality of their spiritual traditions. This is the *social* meaning and purpose of the Findhorn community. It is a significant irony that spiritual teachers from the cultures that have been colonised, and sometimes almost extinguished by our own, the Native Americans, the Aboriginal peoples of Australia and the gurus of India, have become sources of inspiration for an ever-increasing number of people in the 'rich' world, including many members of the community. The export of spiritual wealth is a healthy trade!

Another tenet of the Findhorn community's existence is the acceptance of religious diversity. It must be abundantly clear that the practice of the great fundamental teaching of all religions 'God is Love', 'Love thy neighbour as thyself' is not limited to believers in one religion alone, nor even to those who profess an organised religion at all. Feuding and rejection because of religious belief still remain prevalent all over the globe. Once the meaning of the divine as the indweller in all humanity has been discovered, it is inconceivable to believe that divine truth has been revealed in only one religion or creed. When Jesus says, "I am the Way, the Truth and the

Life," and, "Only through me shall you reach the Kingdom of Heaven," he is talking about the essence of his teaching, which, in the Findhorn community, is called the Christ Consciousness, rather than the particular form that the Christian church has made of it. We are sure that the 'Christ Consciousness' may be as present or absent in Hinduism, Buddhism, Islam, Judaism or even Humanism, as in Christianity, even if different names are used. Sai Baba used to affirm: 'There is only one God He is present everywhere! There is only one race the race of humanity! There is only one religion the religion of Love! There is only one language the language of the heart!' A chosen religion is one personal way to direct one towards that Essence underlying all different forms: our own true nature.

At the Findhorn community people of any religious faith - or none - who are searching for the love that is their inner truth are welcome. The community is open to insights from all religious practices which promote this inner discovery. There are members professing Buddhism, Hinduism, Sufism, those who find inspiration from Native American spirituality, or from esoteric teachings of the so-called 'Western mystery school', as well as Christians. All can get along together, learn from each other, and benefit from the spiritual diversity. This mutual recognition is not a weakening of faith, but a strengthening of it, for we have become citizens of one world. The wealth of each tradition becomes our own heritage as we learn that the essential truth of each religion is the same. Religious forms are like clothes, put on for an individual's personal comfort. Bigots may cavil at this, but the experience of our community shows that where love is, all religious beliefs flourish.

The Generation of Hope

Thinking of the long catalogue of dangers that threaten humanity, it is easy to become despondent, even despairing. Many people share such feelings but suppress them with escapist and nihilistic lifestyles. By living superficially, they try to bypass a pessimistic underlying awareness which feeds their insecurity and anxieties. Sometimes even to bring these feelings to the surface generates great emotional distress, as the community has discovered in hosting workshops on 'deep' ecology.

The experience of living in the Findhorn community transforms this anxiety into hope and anticipation for the future. The discovery that the divine meaning of life is personally available to the seeker is empowering. An awareness grows that all is not moving in a negative direction, the tide can be turned and is being turned. Anyone may be part of this force for change, a 'force' of love that 'conquers' without exercising any violence. By living and learning in this community, we generate hope and excitement, without ignoring the disasters our civilisation creates. Even if we wanted to avoid awareness of the problems that beset our planet, the noise from the military air base nearby until recently reminded us. It was no accident that the Findhorn Foundation was in such close proximity to the base.

Through the guest programmes this hope for change spreads to those who visit. It is not an energy of protest or negation. Though we do not condemn people who take the path of protest, it often tends to entrench reaction, as two energies oppose each other. Usually, little changes, except perhaps in situations which are anyway exceptionally volatile. There is a difference between demonstrating the existence of a problem to those who are not already aware of it, perhaps choosing dramatic means, and actually *solving* that problem. Often protest groups have confused the two and after a while their members become disillusioned and cynical, always in opposition to forces which appear overwhelmingly powerful. Ultimately, it is not what we strive *against* that counts, but what we strive *for*. The method of the Findhorn community is a practical and meaningful one that can be incorporated into the life of any individual inner transformation. Our hopefulness expresses 50 years' experience in the practice of personal spiritual development.

An Ongoing Workshop in Spiritual Education.

The Findhorn community has often been compared to an ongoing workshop, a laboratory for spiritual change. This is partly because people constantly come and go. Guests stay here from a week to several months. Student members stay for a couple of years (depending on the training ideas current at the Foundation) and staff members may stay for several years. There are always new faces, always people starting out as guests or as members. Each newcomer experiences an equivalent process of self-transformation, finds similar blockages and difficulties, and overcomes them. The process of personal change never stops, no matter how long one stays. In the 1989 brochure Eileen Caddy wrote:

Changes are not always comfortable, but they are very necessary if we want to grow and expand. If we stopped going through changes, I would really become concerned because it would mean we were becoming static. That means stagnation, and stagnation means death.

Sometimes the first period within the community is spent with quite a lot of personal drama. Old habits and ideas are exposed and the situation invites their release. Those who stay longer usually become more accepting and graceful about the process, but no one in the community is released from the challenge of personal transformation.

Since life at the Findhorn Foundation is not monastic, it differs from that in the surrounding world only in quality and orientation. Work, relationship and interaction with others occur as in everyday life. But here they are considered an arena for transformation. Situations have a habit of presenting themselves in ways that are exquisitely appropriate to this end. It is very valuable to have a sense of humour to live here; it helps us to appreciate the delightful irony with which events seem to be 'set up'. It is pleasant, when one knows the community well, to stand back and observe the 'Angel of Findhorn', as some call it, at work. Lovingly, the circumstances in which ego is deflated are provided, lifelong attachments are questioned, suppressed emotions are brought to the surface, evasions are countered, and escape from situations is thwarted. As you observe it all, you must smile wryly at the human capacity for self-deception and its transparency. Then you are drawn back once more to be subjected to the same process yourself.

Gradually, the idea of the 'one right way' is released; one learns that what has been invaluable in assisting personal transformation may be anathema to someone else. It is as if we were in a market place with many stalls offering goods. Some people go to one stall to buy, others go to another. We support each other constantly, but the path of inner transformation is ultimately a personal one. However much we may share with others, each of us has a unique path to the Self. The appreciation of this fosters a sense of awe, reverence and humility at the specificity of the Love that is available when we seek to discover it.

In Harmony With the Divine Plan

This small community in northern Scotland, with its special inspiration and apparent divine purpose, does not exist alone. There is a transformation going on all over the planet that is fuelled from many sources. With some of those sources we are directly connected, with others we are not. They have varying emphases and practices, but all are concerned with giving new primacy to inner exploration. We call them a 'network of light', a transformational matrix through which the energy developing the new human identity operates.

In every city small groups have developed, seeking inner change as a means of a new relationship with the world of the senses. If we take them all together and imagine the energy they generate, it is not so difficult to visualise a network of light covering the planet, spreading a new level of human awareness.

Taken together, all this makes up what has been described as the 'new age' movement. Many people are now a little wary of this description, which was once eagerly embraced by the Findhorn community, because in popular thought it has become connected with the sensation seekers satirised in cartoons, whose interest lies less in seeking spiritual transformation than in dabbling in the occult, or in practising classical capitalist entrepreneurship on the naive.

Humanity cannot go back to a religion of custom and tradition, where obedience to the law was simply 'what is done'. Attempts to provide human satisfaction by an appeal to the external senses and the accumulation of possessions have led to a crisis in human history. The Divine will, the energy of creation itself, is steering us in a new direction, towards the discovery of itself within. In time, human beings with a new consciousness may become dominant across the globe. The quicker it actually happens, the less damage will be done, and the less suffering there will be. But the process has to be a real one.

Appendix.

Here is the current 'Common Ground' statement of the Findhorn Foundation Community. Everyone who wants to belong to the community is encouraged to sign this.

"In service to spirit, humanity and the earth we hold in common the following principles, essence and guidelines:-

Principles

Deep inner listening; Co-creation with nature; Love in Action.

Essence

We live in clarity and integrity and seek nothing less than the truth

We live in openness and communion and seek nothing less than communion

We live in gratitude and open-heartedness and seek nothing less than love

We live in courage and willingness and seek nothing less than our soul's path

We live in co-operation and shared vision and seek nothing less than alignment with spirit

We live in awareness and responsibility and seek nothing less than peace

We live in acceptance and surrender and seek nothing less than freedom

Guidelines

1. Spiritual Practice – I have an active spiritual practice to align with spirit and support me to work for the highest good.

2. Service – I bring an attitude of service to others and to our planet, recognizing I must also consider my own needs.

3. Personal Growth – I am committed to the expansion of human consciousness and my own personal growth. I endeavour to recognize and change personal attitudes and behaviour patterns that are limiting.

4. Integrity - I embody congruence of thought, word and action. I take responsibility for the spiritual, environmental and human effects of my actions.

5. Respecting Others – I wholeheartedly respect other people – their differences, views, origins, backgrounds and issues. I respect all forms of life and the Community's and other people's property.

6. Direct Communication - I use clear and honest communication with open listening, heart felt responses, loving acceptance and straightforwardness. I talk to people rather than about them. In public and in private I do not malign or demean others. I may seek helpful advice but do no seek to collude.

7. Reflection – I recognise that anything I see outside myself – any criticisms, irritations or appreciations – may also be reflections of what is inside me, and I commit to looking at these before addressing others.

8. Feedback – I am willing to listen to constructive feed-back and work with it. I offer feedback to others in a caring and appropriate way to challenge and support each other to grow.

9. Non-violence – I do not inflict my attitudes or desires on others. Where appropriate I step in and stop violence, manipulation or intimidation of myself or others, or at least say I would like it to stop.

10. Perspective – For the benefit of the whole community I may need to put aside my personal issues. I acknowledge that there may be wider perspectives than my own and deeper issues than those I am immediately aware of.

11. Co-operation – I clearly communicate my decisions to others who may be affected by them, and consider their views respectfully, I recognise that others may make decisions which affect me, and I respect the care and integrity they have put into their decision-making process.

12. Peacekeeping – I make every effort to resolve disputes. I may call for and advocate, friend, independent observer or mediator to be present, and will use and follow the Community's grievance procedures as necessary.

13. Agreements – I respect the law of the land, keep agreements I have made and do not break or try to evade any Community guidelines.

14. Commitment – I bring the spirit of this statement of Common Ground to all my dealings.

Printed in Poland
by Amazon Fulfillment
Poland Sp. z o.o., Wrocław